America 2020
A Nation in Turmoil

John Stanton

America 2020

ISBN:9798619455953

DEDICATION

For Aaron
&
The Higher Power

CONTENTS

INTRODUCTION

"The US was formed on a very powerful idea... that here in America we will have a government of the people, by the people and for the people. It says that all of the people, regardless if you are male or female [are equal]. It doesn't matter if you are gay or straight or anything in between.

It doesn't matter if you are black or white or Asian or Indian or any other ethnic group. It doesn't matter what the country of your origin is or the spelling of your last name. It does not matter if you are Catholic or Protestant, Muslim or Jew, and it doesn't matter if you believe at all.

It does not matter if you are rich or poor, common or famous. In this country, in these United States, under these colors of red, white and blue, all Americans are created free and equal.

We will rise or fall based on our merit, and we will be judged by the content of our character and not the color of our skin. That is the core organizing principle of the United States of America and that is why we fight." General Mark Milley, USA, former Chief of Staff and now Chairman of the Joint Chiefs of Staff

As I have written elsewhere, there is a critical need for the American people to interact with each other in a civil and civic fashion. There must be a return to the ideals embodied in the US Declaration of Independence, the US Constitution and the Bill of Rights. I still believe strongly in General Mark Milley's remarks on why the US Army fights. Milley is now the Chairman of the Joint Chiefs of Staff and I can only hope that he still believes what he said back in 2017 during a speech to the Association of US Army (AUSA). In the excerpt from his remarks above, he reminded those listening what the United States of America should be, not what it is now. On this course, the shipwreck is immanent.

The reason why the Army fights is also the reason that American civilians, young and old, should fight for a better country. Not with guns and bricks in the street, but through mass political, civic action. Don't like the two party system? Change it. Don't want Social Security and Medicaid privatized?

Stop it. Think politicians are overusing the US military? Tell them to grow a spine and stop hiding behind the military. In the end, the needs of community and country must surpass ideology, party affiliation and tribe.

Americans should remember that soldiers, sailors, airmen and Marines want to be part of a country that not only strives to be better each day, but that functions as a great country should. That means taking care of its people and infrastructure, and bolstering the laws and institutions that guard against tyranny and madness within the government and society.

There are no market based solutions for those tasks. Milley's remarks remind us all what kind of nation and people we should be.

America 2020—A Nation in Turmoil— is a collection of observations on the US State of the Union in 2020. With political polarization perhaps approaching its zenith, a presidential election will take place in November 2020 that will pit incumbent Donald Trump against a right leaning democrat like former vice president Joe Biden or the democratic socialist Bernie Sanders.

As it is, the Republican party has been overtaken by rightest zealots whose ideology is nothing but fealty to Trump, corporate interests and the destruction of social programs.

Trump has exposed the Democrats as little more than a moderate version of Trump--if there is such a creature--whose interests largely coincide with Trump's brand of republicanism. Because of this, millions of workers who occupy positions in various class structures; young and old; Black, White, Brown; LGBTQ appear to be moving to a more progressive, American brand of democratic socialism. Sanders has put into motion forces that the centrist and rightist Republicans and Democrats do not favor.

Sanders opponents simply do not want to share the wealth of the nation with all. His movement, even if he fails, will only grow stronger and be a force to be reckoned with in the next presidential election, maybe even the mid-term congressional elections in a couple of years.

As Norbert Wiener once remarked, "In a very real sense, we are shipwrecked passengers on a doomed planet. Yet, even in a shipwreck, human decencies and human values do not necessarily vanish, and we must make the most of them. We shall go down, but let it be in a manner to which we may look forward as worthy of our dignity."

That is something worth remembering.

How the World Ends: A Story

I'm writing this letter to myself. I need to talk to someone, even if it is only my own self. I need to believe that what happened was real.

All that I know of the past was learned by word-of-mouth histories from those who came before me and those few historians who remain now. Some matters I know directly. We don't talk much anymore to each other because it takes too much physical effort. It has been tiring to write this letter by the dim light available to me either in or outdoors, day or night. But it helps to distract me from the situation everyone is in.

I was part of the BMR or the Baltimore Metro Resistance. I was part of the BMR when I was young and I guess I still am a member now. My parents migrated to Baltimore from Virginia. They are gone now, killed in fighting by bullet, blade, bomb, artillery or missile. That's what I was told. I often wish now that I would have died with them, such are the circumstances these days.

There were other resistance groups in the former United States of America that I know of: Los Angeles, Houston, New Orleans, Saint Louis, Chicago, Detroit, Boston, New York City, Philadelphia, Charlotte (North Carolina) and Miami. Millions flocked to these locations in hopes of defending themselves from the brutal federal and state militaries; para-military security forces and mercenaries, and local police.

When I was very young, I became a courier in the BMR transporting everything from letters, food, ammunition, tools, medicine, water. I eventually became a competent, adaptable fighter with about an average talent for writing. There were so many thousands of us that were BMR fighters but only about 100 of us at any one time had the responsibility to compose three page letters that would serve as a narrative of the day or night's activity. The letters included stories of combat, the details of terrain, retreat or advance, stalemates and casualties, poems, puzzles, trivia, anything that could be read for a few moments of escape. Once composed the many letters written by all of us went into a zip lock plastic bag, and circulated throughout our metro area for reading.

War

War does funny things, I suppose, like bringing people together or tearing them apart or both. In tearing apart the United States, the government, clearly not intending to do so, brought people together, at least in our case. Our BMR was made up of black, white, latino, asian, and mixed race fighters, young and old, LGBTQ, anyone who accepted our cause. History, race, ethnicity or class no longer mattered to any of us. Sure, there were leaders and order necessary for operations, everyone below a leader was trained in how and when to fight and with what. Tactics and strategy did not belong to an elite particularly since no one could afford to be located at a central command post.

The only reference points in time I have for a starting point for the emergence of the resistance groups, or I suppose city-states, is 2020 to 2045. Beyond that, I don't know whether it is now late in the 21 St Century or early in 22nd Century. Our oral historians told us that, at least in the then United States, martial law was declared during those years and the US Constitution and Bill of Rights were suspended. Government pensions, medical benefits, food assistance, environmental protections and every form of civilian aid were suspended apparently in about 2025 by presidential order. Elections were also suspended with the president appointing those who he thought should represent the people. Tribunals took the place of courts. A few other presidents came and went, I was told, but the die was cast: the allure of power was too much for anyone to care about the general populace.

These were frantic times in the BMR as everyone knew an attack by government forces was imminent. But with the number of metro areas offering refuge and armed resistance, plus the ongoing wars the government was waging overseas, there would have to be careful planning by the enemy military leaders. Our strategists and tacticians reminded us that high ranking government military commanders were plodding, conventional thinkers bound up in the false promises of technology.

I learned that during the initial setup of the BMR, major food and clothing chains, drug stores, camping and fishing outlets, boats docked of any type, fuel from gas stations, water sources, weapons of all types from gun shops and ammunition all took part in emptying their shelves and stocking all the goods at various hardened sites in the BMR. Bank vaults, below ground parking garages and wherever there was a below ground facility were stocked. Prepositioned stocks of weapons, ammo and food were stored outside the Baltimore City limits. Shipping containers loaded with canned goods or plastic water bottles were submerged in the Baltimore harbor.

Tunnel construction began in earnest, tiered defenses were setup for BMR's inner, outer and suburban areas. Choke points were set that would funnel attackers into kill zones. Booby traps, crude land-mines and even crossbows were used during the fight. Bicycles and skateboards were put to good use since fuel was severely rationed. Methods of communication had to be devised that would not emit heat because they would be detected by electronic warfare packages on enemy aircraft. We had to devise a low flying drone defense and we had to find a way to hide critical weapons and stores from satellites. Again, we lucked out because a lot of satellite and drone time was allocated by the government forces to their overseas conflicts.

Advantages

We had the good fortune to have in the BMR Johns Hopkins medical and research personnel on our side along with most of the air and space staff moving in with us from Goddard space flight center not far away. Many from nearby Fort Meade and some from the former National Security Agency joined us. I am not sure of the functions of many of those people but I know that doctors, technologists, space researchers and weapons developers were among them. We were able to develop our own drones that were used for reconnaissance.

I have heard that nearly 40 percent of those forces joined the resistance bringing with them weapons, munitions, vehicles and, more importantly, training. I learned too that some Virginia Class Submarines, three strategic ballistic missile nuke submarines, a handful of AEGIS warships, and even one Carrier Strike Group joined the resistance too.

Of those, two Virginia Class attack submarines joined the BMR along with two AEGIS warships. Initially, no one in the BMR was sure what to do with this firepower but it didn't take long for the technologists and military personnel that came ashore to suggest good use of the Navy vessels.The one SSBN that was aligned with the BMR may have served as a deterrent to the government nuking us. But it and one of the two Virginia attack class subs would have to take to the deep ocean to be effective. I did not learn of their fate. We were not nuked, I know that.

The other attack submarine that stayed with us had a nuclear power source. I don't understand how they did it (though we did have some pretty smart people in our camp) but they were able to move the nuclear power source to a facility deep within the BMR. I guess the idea was to use it to power a BMR of the future. I'm not sure what came of that effort though in the end it didn't matter.

The Virginia attack sub arrived to us loaded with cruise missiles and a couple of Navy SEAL units. The SEALS would push back an attack by other Navy SEALS dispatched by submersible from pro-government submarines to infiltrate and terrorize the BMR. They were essential to our defense and raiding/scouting efforts.

Cruise missiles were fired from our Virginia attack sub and I think they found their way to artillery and tank emplacements that initially surrounded us. The AEGIS warships managed to fend off some aircraft and missile attacks but ultimately succumbed to anti-ship missiles homing in on their heat signatures. The sub was eventually sunk by torpedo, I think.

Lucky

We figured we had a fighting chance against our opponents but make no mistake: it was because events were taking place outside the United States that might make our struggle successful. It is one thing to quell an internal rebellion, quite another to succeed against 100 million resistance fighters tucked away in metro areas while trying to win wars in foreign lands, on and below the world's oceans, and in space. We figured that our opponents would eventually run short of fuel and munitions with so many to fight and we, luckily, were right.

Still, like all the other resistance groups around in the former United States and around the world , we lost thousands and thousands during the relentless barrages from air, sea and land. We started out poorly in defending the BMR on the ground but after fits and starts managed to push back our enemies. We learned that the Miami, Florida and Charlotte, North Carolina BMRs were defeated. Both Florida and North Carolina had a heavy government military presence and even with the help of those in the military that came to the aid of the resistance it wasn't enough.

We celebrated the cessation of fighting for a short time. We all were skeptical that it was really over but our scouting parties found abandoned tanks, vehicles, artillery pieces and a lot of dead and decaying bodies. The peace was short lived. Then nukes came. And then the planet rebelled.

During some short time period, some fateful decisions were made by the former United States, Russia, Pakistan, India and China.

Who knows the sequence but the end result was horrifying. I guess the first thing to say was that China decided that US Pacific fleet forces, the three Carrier Strike Groups there, were vulnerable. China decided to take on those forces with their conventional forces and suffered badly. The Chinese surface, subsurface and air forces were largely destroyed. Given that hundreds of millions of their own people were fighting their People's Liberation Army within their own borders the vaunted advantage of PLA ground forces vanished. With their naval forces destroyed by the United States and Pacific allies, they decided to launch nuclear weapons at Japan, Okinawa, Guam and Taiwan where the US fleet had a presence. The same weapons were launched at the three carrier groups in the China area of operations with the result being the elimination of US forces.

At the same time. Russia decided that the time was ripe for moving further into Ukraine, the Baltic's and Europe, into a barely armed Germany. Meager NATO forces supported by sacrificial US support units were no match for the Russians. Seeing defeat, the US launched scores of tactical nukes to stop the onslaught. At the same time, India and Pakistan decided to settle their scores by launching their stock of nukes at each other. Nuclear warheads flew between those two countries and around the globe. We learned that Newport News, San Diego, sub bases on the East and west coasts of the United States were destroyed by nukes. Washington, DC, Houston and New

Orleans were also eliminated. Ground based missiles anywhere in the world, in our case in the Northwest, were cratered by nukes turning those places into radioactive no go zones.

The Nukes Time ended. Our skies were psychedelic with colors that defied sense. Orange, gray, blue, yellow, black colors would appear each day. It was getting cold as the sun seemed to fade into the distance. Our Geiger counters registered high but tolerable radiation. But many of us started feeling sick.

We learned, thanks to our telecommunications, internet and satellite technicians that the scene was the same all over the planet. Populations of the former United States, Russia, China, India, Pakistan Europe, Brazil, Malaysia, Mexico Indonesia, the African nations, were all now displaced moving by sea or land in hopes of surviving somewhere.

After the Nuke Time there was another calm period. Many of us were worried about this. We had all forgotten about Climate Change and planetary disturbances.

Earth Revolts

I remember one day waking up in the BMR thinking that the Earth had fallen away under me. I learned that the West Coast earthquake had finally come putting Los Angeles and the West Coast of the United States into the Pacific ocean. The volcano that was said to be dormant in the Pacific northwest exploded sending soot and tremors throughout the former United States. It was undeniable that the Earth said Enough! There were earthquakes and subsequent Tsunamis. Volcanic eruptions around the Earth were so severe that the sky turned black.

Snowflakes made of ash fell from the sky. Respiratory distress was the norm. People coughed so hard that they vomited blood.

Probably the worst image of the times was picked up by a couple of our drones roaming over Ocean City, Maryland. Marine life started to appear on the beaches dead or dying. Thousands of people mauled each other and the dead, beached creatures for something to eat. The video was awful particularly since we knew that anyone eating the toxic meat from the oceans would have convulsions and vomiting with 24 hours and would die. The worst thing we saw from these video feeds was that people slaughtered each other for what they thought was good food.

All the coastal cities in the world are gone, sunk into the oceans. The oceans have turned into some viscous polluted mass. The seas and vicious weather pursue us up into the high ground or wherever we go.

I am ending this letter. I will drink a pint of vodka, take many opioids and go into the black. But before that, I will put this letter into the zip lock bag and bury it somewhere.

****

Sir.

Yes, what is it.

Our sentient droids scattered around and above this planet have uploaded our data for analyses into the primary ship.

Good.

Make sure that all the sentient programming on this planet is uploaded back into the bio machinery. There is much to analyze.

Of course, sir.

Sir, one of our archeo devices has come across what appears to be a first hand account of the demise of this planet.

Good, construct it, translate it and send it to me.

Yes.

Are you ok ,sir?

Yes, this narrative is very sad, moving even. Well, put this in the archives with the other data retrieved from this planet.

Again, do not leave any of our sentient programs in this place. Send out warning satellites outside the ring of debris that surrounds this planet. Send out a warning using universal Planck communications that this place is toxic.

Let us move out of this solar system

Time for an American Brand of Democratic Socialism: Erich Fromm's The Sane Society Offers Guidance

"His value as a person lies in his salability, not in his human qualities of love, reason, or in his artistic capacities. Happiness becomes identical with consumption of newer and better commodities, the drinking in of music, screen plays, fun, sex, liquor and cigarettes. Not having a sense of self except the one which conformity with the majority can give, he is insecure, anxious, depending on approval. He is alienated from himself, worships the product of his own hands, the leaders of his own making, as if they were above him, rather than made by him. He is in a sense back where he was before the great human evolution began in the second Millennium BC. He is incapable of love and to use his reason, to make decisions, in fact incapable to appreciate life and thus ready and even willing to

destroy everything. The world is again fragmented, has lost its unity; he is again worshiping diversified things, with the only exception that now they are man-made, rather than part of nature."

"The facts, however, are that the modern, alienated individual has opinions and prejudices but no convictions, has likes and dislikes, but no will. His opinions and prejudices, likes and dislikes, are manipulated in the same way as his tastes, by powerful propaganda machines—which might not be effective were he not already conditioned to such influences by advertising and by his whole alienated way of life. The average voter is poorly informed too. While he reads his newspaper regularly, the whole world is so alienated from him that nothing makes real sense or carries real meaning. He reads of billions of dollars being spent, of millions of people being killed; figures, abstractions, which are in no way interpreted in a concrete, meaningful picture of the world. The science fiction he reads

is little different from the science news. Everything is unreal, unlimited, impersonal. Facts are so many lists of memory items, like puzzles in a game, not elements on which his life and that of his children depends. we come across a person who acts and feels like an automaton; who never experiences anything which is really his; who experiences himself entirely as the person he thinks he is supposed to be; whose artificial smile has replaced genuine laughter; whose meaning-less chatter has replaced communicative speech; whose dulled despair has taken the place of genuine pain."

"Suppose that in our Western culture movies, radios, television, sports events and newspapers ceased to function for only four weeks. With these main avenues of escape closed, what would be the consequence for people thrown back upon their own resources? I have no doubt that even in this short time thousands of nervous breakdowns would occur, and many more thousands of people would be

thrown into a state of acute anxiety, not different from the picture which is diagnosed clinically as neurosis. " Erich Fromm, *The Sane Society*, 1955

++++

The derisive children's sandbox terms used by media pundits, Democratic and Republican stooges and the One Percent to describe Senator Bernie Sanders of Vermont, a millionaire himself, would be comedic if it were not so sad. The words used to denigrate Sanders would be instantly recognized by Fromm since they were used in 1955 in the same fashion during the first Cold War.

Sanders, a self proclaimed Democratic Socialist, is, in fact, not the demon that nuts like MSNBC's Chris Matthews claim him to be. According to the publication The Hill, Matthews compared Sander's to the Nazis. That's interesting because, according to The Hill, "Sanders is Jewish and most of his family members were killed in the Holocaust.”

Antisemitism anyone?

What is a Democratic Socialist?

Fromm describes a Democratic Socialist as one who believes this:

“ We cannot afford to lose any of the fundamental achievements of modern democracy--either the fundamental one of representative government, that is, government elected by the people and responsible to the people, or any of the rights which the Bill of Rights guarantees to every citizen. Nor can we compromise the newer democratic principle that no one shall be allowed to starve, that society is responsible for all its members, that no one shall be frightened into submission and lose his human pride through fear of unemployment and starvation.

These basic achievements must not only be preserved; they must be fortified and expanded. In spite of the fact that this measure of democracy has been realized-- though far from completely--it is not enough. Progress for democracy lies in enhancing the actual freedom, initiative, and spontaneity of the individual, not only in certain private and spiritual matters, but above all in the activity fundamental to every man's existence, his work. What are the general conditions for that? The irrational and plan-less character of society must be replaced by a planned economy that represents the planned and concerted effort of society as such. Society must master the social problem as rationally as it has mastered nature. One condition for this is the elimination of the secret rule of those who, though few in number, wield great economic power without any responsibility to those whose fate depends on their decisions. "

We may call this new order by the name of democratic socialism but the name does not matter; all that matters is that we establish a rational economic system serving the purposes of the people."

With the United States devolving into some sort of weird corporate fascist state, isn't it time to get back on track toward evolving towards a progressive, stable, all-inclusive, well-defended union? America is going the wrong way. Hell will not be pleasant.

I Like the F-35: I Get High on the Jobs it Creates for Vermont

Let's take a brief look at Sander's voting record.

He voted to confirm General David Petraeus, (USA, Ret.) to run operations in the Middle East area of operations. He voted "yes" on funding wars in Iraq and Afghanistan, unemployment benefits extensions for veterans of those wars, and enhancing the GI Bill's benefits. He also voted for funding for a border fence and security along the US-Mexico border. He supports jobs programs, infrastructure improvements, national health insurance and the repeal of President Donald Trump's tax cut.

The National Interest reported that Sanders supported the deployment of F-35's to Vermont because it's a great jobs program for the tiny state and its National Guard Unit was eager to get the aircraft. The publication cited figures that showed that constructing components for the F-35, (its bomb bays and the aircraft's Gatling Gun) in Vermont accounts for 1600 jobs and roughly $222 million in economic activity

While Trump's fascist and racist tendencies have made mincemeat out of the traditional, moderate Republican Party into a bunch of Trump ring-kissers, he has also exposed the centrist and right wing elements of the Democratic Party for what it is: A quiet partner in Trump's assault on immigrants, social programs, and whopping increases in the US defense budget. Its rightward tilt matches the Republican swing in the same direction. No where is that more evident in the desiccated, flip-flopping, right wing leaning Joe Biden (Democrat), put up by Democratic Party leaders as a viable presidential candidate. Yuck!

Alexandria Ocasio-Cortez, a Sanders disciple, is the long term future of what remains of the Democratic Party; that is, if she doesn't start a new, progressive party that breaks with one head of the two headed monster. Her voting record includes support for not allowing Russia back into the G7 groups of nations until it gets out of Ukraine; and, on another piece of legislation, voted "yes" to stopping Trump from reducing funding for NATO. Her voting record matches Sanders in many instances.

Cold War 2020: Nukes and Propaganda

The timing of the attacks by the Democratic and Republican party vanguard coincides neatly with the "new reality" of Great Power Competition with China and Russia, which the Pentagon and denizens of in the mainstream media—and Washington, DC's many Thinks Tanks—are pushing. With the trillion dollars to be spent on the nuclear Triad modernization, the current deployment of low yield nuclear weapons on some US Navy submarines—and the open talk of using nuclear weapons, if only in a simulation, by the Secretary of Defense, Mark Esper, you'd think the US is heading back to the Cold War mentality of 1955. Perhaps is time to replay Stanley Kubrick's classic movie *Dr. Strangelove or How I learned to Stop Worrying and Love the Bomb.*

That means that language has to accompany the shift to fighting the Stalinist Commies/Socialists in Russia and China. In the coming months and years, US propagandists will have to create an atmosphere of fear in the general public not unlike was done for the War on Terror, and Saddam Hussein's regime in Iraq in the lead up to both wars waged by the US on that hapless country.

The terms Left and Democratic Socialist will become equated with sympathy for China and Russia; support for repeal of tax cuts for corporations and the wealthy; fighting for funding of food stamp programs and environmental protections; the protection of Social Security, Medicare/Medicaid; and pushing for healthcare-for-all and employment insurance.

Those attacks must be pushed back by coalitions like the one Sanders has worked so hard to build. Ocasio-Cortez, and those like her, will have to carry the torch once Sanders passes it on to them. The young men and women of the United States are critical in building a Democratic Socialist front.

The End?

With all the talk of Artificial Intelligence, robotics and its dangers in war and peace, plus the ominous consequences of Synthetic Biology gone wrong, it's worth closing with a comment by Fromm on the matter. The world is always looking for modern-day thinkers to divine the future. But that's already been done by real intellectuals like Erich Fromm. He was right on many aspects of Democratic Socialism (though not on a total command economy) and below is his take on the future of humanity written in 1955. I fear he may be right.

"In the nineteenth century the problem was that God is dead; in the twentieth [and 21st] century the problem is that man is dead. In the nineteenth century inhumanity meant cruelty; in the twentieth [and 21st] century it means schizoid self-alienation. The danger of the past was that men became slaves. The danger of the future is that men may become robots. True enough, robots do not rebel. But given man's nature, robots cannot live and remain sane, they become Golems, they will destroy their world and themselves because they cannot stand any longer the boredom of a meaningless life."

The USA's System of Checks, Balances and Reality Crumbles as it Seeks War with Iran: Send in Pope Francis, Not the Marines

"Any Muslim who denies JesusChrist's and Saint Mary's infallibility is rejected by Islam. This is how Islam respects Jesus and Mary (pbut). The honor Muslims attribute to #JesusChrist (pbuh) is no less than his position and merit in the eyes of the Christian believers in Christianity. Today, many who claim to follow Jesus Christ, take a different path than that of him. The guidance of #Jesus, the son of #Mary (peace be upon our Prophet and her) is guidance towards worshiping God and confronting the Pharaohs and tyrants. Following JesusChrist requires adherence to righteousness and abhorrence of anti-righteous powers, and it is hoped that Christians and #Muslims in every part of the world will adhere to this great lesson from Jesus (pbuh) in their lives and deeds." Ayatollah Khamenei, Supreme Leader

Yes, boys and girls, he did say that and if you visit Khamenei's Twitter site you'll find him sitting next to an elderly woman and to the right of her a Christmas tree adorned with ornaments including one of Santa Claus. And did you know, kiddies, that Iran's Majles, the equivalent of the UK's House of Commons or the US House of Representatives (one hates to make that comparison to denigrate the Majles) has reserved, by constitutional decree/law—dating to 1906, five seats for the following minorities: two Christian Armenians, one Assyrian-Chaldean Christian, one Jew and one Zoroastrian. The Ayatollah Kohmenei preserved the condition after the Iranian revolution of 1979. This according to the United States Institute for Peace (USIP—link above).

It is interesting to note what USIP has to say about the Majles/ Parliament and its relations with the Iranian presidency, the Supreme Leader and the Guardian Council. "The 290-member parliament is weak compared with the presidency, as well as with the non-elected institutions such as the 12-member Guardian Council and the supreme leader's office."

The US House of Representatives and the US Senate are, indeed, weak compared with the US presidency and let us substitute "non-elected institutions" with the Department of Defense, lobbyists, campaign financiers and the two-party corporate media monsters (reflecting Democrats and Republicans) run by Disney, Comcast, NewsCorp, and so on.

Supreme Leader's Veto = US President's Veto

And it turns out, according to the USIP, that the Majles has its own troubles with the Supreme Leaders use of a veto to thwart its legislative power. Though not arising out of the Iranian president's office, it is in effect vetoing parliament's legislation or proposed legislation. "Parliament has faced other obstacles. The supreme leader's office has intervened in the legislative process through a mechanism called the "state order." The supreme leader's most controversial intervention was in mid-2000, when he ordered a bill proposing to reform Iran's repressive press laws be removed from the docket."

Oh, what a flimsy comparison! But wait. Trump's Guardian Council (Secretary of Defense Mark Esper, Secretary of State Mike Pompeo, CIA Director Gina Haspel and Chair of the Joint Chiefs of Staff Gen. Mark Milley) recently told two US Republican senators that they should not debate legislation to limit President Donald Trump's power to go to war with Iran. The US officials were sent to the House and Senate on Wednesday to brief legislators on the rationale for killing Iranian General Soleimani.

"GOP Sens. Mike Lee (Utah) and Rand Paul (Ky.) ripped the administration over a closed-door briefing on Iran on Wednesday, announcing they will now support a resolution reining in President Trump's military powers. Lee, speaking to reporters after a roughly hour long closed-door meeting with administration officials, characterized it as ' the worst briefing I've seen, at least on a military issue. Lee said the officials warned that Congress would embolden Iran if lawmakers debated Trump's war powers. 'I find this insulting and demeaning ... to the office that each of the 100 senators in this building happens to hold. I find it insulting and demeaning to the Constitution of the United States.' Lee did not say which briefer made the assertion but specified that no administration representative contradicted them."

On paper the United States Constitution, specifically the checks and balances system adopted by the framers (from Montesquieu) was intended to keep the three branches as co-equals. It seems that James Madison, at least, was wrong about controlling factionalism. Polarization/factionalism, in the form of the corrupted US two party system, has nearly destroyed the Republic. The executive branch is overpowering—no matter what party holds office (at least since George W. Bush)—the US Congress seems only as powerful as the party that holds the presidency and the judiciary is loaded up with whatever conservative or liberal ideologues the president sees fit to appoint. (For an interesting read on how the US political process should be changed see UK's need to be change, see A.C. Grayling: Democracy and Its Crisis.)

Trump's Response to Iran's Missiles Hitting US Bases in Iraq

Looking at a still photo of Trump giving his "morning after speech" on the Iranian missile strike I wasn't sure if I was hallucinating or not. There was Trump behind the podium dressed up like Mussolini. On one side of Trump was Vice President Mike Pence dressed in a Nazi uniform. The stone faced members of the US Joint Chiefs of Staff, proving that the United States is way ahead in the development of

Artificial Intelligence appeared to me as Terminators. I had wondered if someone stuck a pin into Secretary of State Mike Pompeo that he would deflate like a balloon.

Well, the World Socialists hit the nail on the head in describing the troublesome scene and the content, or lack thereof, in his remarks.

"Much of what Trump had to say was recycled from previous speeches and tweets denouncing and slandering both Iran and General Qassem Suleimani. But more important than anything that Trump said was the way in which his speech was staged. In an unprecedented violation of constitutional protocol, Trump addressed the nation flanked by the entire uniformed Joint Chiefs of Staff as well as Vice President Mike Pence, Secretary of State Mike Pompeo and Secretary of Defense Mark Esper. On all previous occasions, the announcement of a major crisis or a military engagement has been made by a president, seated at his desk in the Oval Office. This image was intended to present Trump as the leader of a military junta...

Why did Trump fail to act on his threats? It is more than likely that the Joint Chiefs of Staff warned Trump that precipitous action could result in a military disaster.

The Pentagon needs time to prepare the defense of some 70,000 US troops deployed on Iran's borders from Afghanistan to Turkey, along with tens of thousands more military contractors and naval personnel stationed in the region. The military knows that the next round of US attacks will probably be answered with a rain of Iranian missiles on US bases, airfields, battleships and aircraft carriers. In the run-up to the US wars against Iraq in 1990 and 2003, Washington needed several months to prepare against a far less potent enemy.

There are also political considerations by Washington's war planners. More time is needed to develop pro-war propaganda and psychologically condition the population for levels of violence unknown since the end of World War II. This propaganda will include efforts to condition the American people to accept the use of nuclear weapons by the United States, with the assistance of the pliant corporate media. The mass protests in Iran and throughout the Middle East, provoked by Suleimani's killing, provided an indication of the upheavals that will be unleashed by an all-out US war…"

In looking at the video as Trump walked down a corridor to deliver his remarks was that the two US generals nearest to the door were facing each other. As soon as Trump walked by they turned and faced the camera's. Perhaps military protocol, but in these dangerous times with a demagogue in the Oval Office, it was nonetheless unsettling.

OK Boys and Girls: Why the US Can't Win a Conventional War with Iran

Let us dispense immediately with who has more blood on their hands, The United States or Iran. Well, there the Iran-Iraq War during which the US supported Iraq even as it used chemical weapons on Iranians. There is the Saudi campaign in Yemen, which the US supports, which has caused one of the worst humanitarian disasters of the last decade. Then there is that little piece of history from 1953 during which the United States and the UK overthrew the Iranian government. And remember this: No matter what the circumstance, United States is the victim, it's always the victim; in fact, it is exceptional in its victimhood having never been the transgressor or having caused any group or nation to seek reprisal or recompense.

The first matter to note is that Iran has observer status in the Shanghai Cooperation Organization (SCO) which is an alliance between China, Russia, India, Pakistan, Tajikistan, Uzbekistan, Kyrgyzstan and Kazakhstan. As the Wiki entry noted, "In 2017, SCO's eight full members account for approximately half of the world's population, a quarter of the world's GDP, and about 80% of Eurasia's landmass." As Iran remains under US sanctions, it is prohibited from becoming a full member adds another minor reason why Iran is under perpetual economic sanctions by the USA.

Iran is directly bordered by Azerbaijan, Armenia, Turkey, Iraq, Pakistan and Afghanistan. Iran has maritime borders with Bahrain, Kuwait, Oman, Saudi Arabia, and the United Arab Emirates.

The distance between the capitals of Iran and Saudi Arabia, separated by the Persian Gulf, by air, is roughly 788 miles, well within reach of each other's ballistic missiles. Iran is twice the size of Texas with more mountainous terrain.

Relations between Iran and its neighbors are up and down. According to the CIA Factbook (which correctly notes Iran's non-compliance with human trafficking standards), "Iran protests Afghanistan's limiting flow of dammed Helmand River tributaries during drought; Iraq's lack of a maritime boundary with Iran prompts jurisdiction disputes beyond the mouth of the Shatt al Arab in the Persian Gulf; Iran and UAE dispute Tunb Islands and Abu Musa Island, which are occupied by Iran; Azerbaijan, Kazakhstan, and Russia ratified Caspian seabed delimitation treaties based on equidistance, while Iran continues to insist on a one-fifth slice of the sea; Afghan and Iranian commissioners have discussed boundary monument densification and resurvey."

Iran and Azerbaijan have a testy relationship with one another. Armenian analyst Tevan Poghosyan said recently that,"Against the backdrop of US-Iran conflict, Azerbaijan has become a platform for pressure on Iran from the US and Israel, from which unmanned aerial vehicles are being launched toward the Islamic Republic."

Armenia and Iran appear to have cordial bilateral relations and profitable tourism and trade between each other. Armenia has said it will remain neutral in the Iran-US conflict. The same appears true of Turkmenistan and Iran. It is no surprise that Iran and Afghanistan have closer relations than one would normally associate with a US puppet regime. But Afghanistan and Teheran are strong trading partners despite the influx of Afghani immigrants and refugees into Iran due to the ongoing US-Iraqi military operations against the Taliban and Islamic State. This has caused friction between the Iranian and Afghanistan governments.

Iran and Turkey's relations are determined largely by the United States. Though trade and tourism continue, Turkey no longer purchases oil/gas from Iran due to economic sanctions.

Iran and Pakistan relations are beset with problems. According to TRTWorld's Tom Hussein, "For Afghanistan and Pakistan, the alarming escalation of tensions between their common neighbour Iran and the US, their shared geopolitical overlord, could not have come at a worse time.Since the Islamic revolution, however, Pakistan has aligned itself with Saudi Arabia, while at the same time pleading neutrality in the hostility between Riyadh and Tehran. Unsurprisingly, this approach has backfired repeatedly, with terrible consequences... Pakistan flatly refused to join the Saudi-led military coalition that invaded Yemen in 2015, after Iranian-backed Houthi rebels seized most of the country. This infuriated Riyadh and Abu Dhabi, but the benefits to Islamabad's relationship with Tehran were short-lived. Shortly after Imran Khan took power as prime minister in August 2018, Pakistan sought to repair the damage to its relations with the Gulf Arabs and invited the Saudis to set up an oil refinery complex at the Chinese-operated port of Gwadar, located close to the Iranian border. Since then, cross border attacks by militant separatists on both sides have been on the rise. Fear of a serious escalation prompted talks between Iran's political leaders and Pakistan's powerful military in November."

Stir it all Up and What Do You Get?

There are simply too many military fronts for the US/NATO to handle simultaneously, particularly on the ground. Even with the Saudi's and Kuwaiti's as allies, one has to doubt those two nation's fighting capabilities in any ground conflict. US military units can't count on the Saudi's or Kuwait's turning against them during combat.

The US Army and Marines would face ground attacks from within Syria and Iraq and, of course, upon entering Iran they'd find it's not Iraq circa 2003. US troops in Afghanistan would also find themselves, if not in retreat, then under constant attack. Who knows what new "terrorist" alliances would be made. A neo-Islamic State perhaps, joining up with other anti-US forces.

Refugee camps along the Pakistan-Afghnistan-Iran borders would be a hotbed for militias recruiting for the campaign against the Great Satan. The Iranian's have learned well that the United States and its military are very predictable in order of attack: massive, world wide propaganda campaigns to include trumped up cyberattacks on US commercial interests; air-land-sea-space assets redeployed; cruise missile strikes, followed by aircraft bombing runs. US Combat Controllers will have already Halo Jumped into remote portions of Iran to setup staging areas before any invasion starts.

The Navy and Air Force must make quick work of their Iranian equivalents because airpower will be needed to protect US ground troops in multi-theaters of operation from getting overrun from many directions by militias (Pakistan, Afghanistan) or Iranian troops allied with those who will come to its defense. The SCO will have something to say about the matter too. Will Russia and China provide support to the Iranians? Will Russia and China figure that they might as well go toe-to-toe with the US now before it completes nuclear modernization (and in light of the new military strategy of Great Power Competition).

The US Marines and Army will have it the toughest. They may try a WWII style-beach landing onto Iranian shores from the Persian Gulf using US Marines and US Army paratroopers may attempt to come from the sky into Iranian territory. As with any war between the US and North Korea, tactical nukes will have to be considered by the United States. Sides will be chosen and it will be a bloodbath, just as overtaking North Korea would.

Time to call Pope Francis. Given how crazy the times are, it's a good idea.

The Price of Participating in Society is the Sacrifice of Privacy and Self

In what is arguably one of the most craven opportunistic moves by a business/media group to increase its circulation/profitability, on 10 April the New York Times (NYT) embarked on what it describes as its *Privacy Project*. A day later on 11 April, no doubt with the NYT's foreknowledge of what was to come thanks to an unofficial US government tip, Ecuador revoked Julian Assange's (Wikileaks founder) asylum in its UK Embassy and fed him to the British Police dogs eagerly awaiting to arrest him and dump him in jail.

In May 2017 *I wrote* that Assange was doomed from the get-go to be arrested and handed over to the US Government and that it would only be a matter of time before Edward Snowden befell a similar fate.

"*Chelsea Manning's* leaked *information made WikiLeaks and its founder, Julian Assange, a household name. It also made them permanent enemies of the US State. In 2010, Assange released a video that he called Collateral Murder. The video shows an airstrike in which Iraqi journalists are killed. Other releases based on Manning's leak were known as the Afghan Diary and Iraq War Logs. The diplomatic cables exposed some of the silly machinations of the US State Department and the over classification of documents.*

Meanwhile, mainstream media (MSM) outlets like the New York Times and Washington Post feasted on the leaks and gave them prominent coverage daily, even as they excoriated Assange and his merry band of leakers. The MSM believes that WikiLeaks is not "real" journalism even as they used the classified material Assange provided to bolster their subscription numbers. Aren't they accessories to Assange's crime? Apparently they are not.

Assange has been living for the past five years under diplomatic protection in the Embassy of Ecuador in the United Kingdom. He has been accused of rape in Sweden and, if he leaves the embassy, would be arrested by UK authorities and, ultimately, end up in the USA. To make matters worse, now he is a target of the Central Intelligence Agency (CIA) director.

Pompeo once praised WikiLeaks. Whatever data he has seen that made him go ballistic can't be good for Assange, obviously. [Former] Attorney General Jefferson Beauregard Sessions over at the Justice Department has hinted that an arrest warrant is in the works.

He will never get a get out of jail card and is trapped in Ecuador's Embassy in London. The trip from the UK to Sweden to the USA would be swift if he capitulates. 'It's time to call out WikiLeaks for what it really is: A non-state, hostile intelligence service often abetted by state actors like Russia,' [then] CIA director Mike Pompeo said at a May event hosted by the Center for Strategic and International Studies in Washington, DC. 'Assange is a narcissist who has created nothing of value and he relies on the dirty work of others to make himself famous: He's a fraud.'

Assange continues to dig a hole for himself with the CIA Vault leaks even as he enlightens us all, apparently, about the machinations of governments around the world."

Hello Clipper

The New York Times Privacy Project's mission statement is essentially a rehash of a privacy and encryption issue that began on 16 April 1993 over the National Security Agency's proposal to embed a *Clipper Chip* in the nation's communications networks and nascent Internet/World Wide Web (WWW). The chip would have allowed NSA and US Law Enforcement Agencies like the Federal Bureau of Investigation to easily access foreign and domestic public communications. The proposal was the brainchild of President Bill Clinton's administration but a wide awake American public and anti-Clipper Chip groups like the Electronic Frontier Foundation (EFF) opposed the technology and by 1996 the US government gave up on the technology.

There is grave doubt whether the American public or pro-Assange interest groups have the voice and staying power of those like the EFF that a couple of decades ago opposed the Clipper Chip.

According to the New York Times project mission statement,*"The boundaries of privacy are in dispute, and its future is in doubt. Citizens, politicians and business leaders are asking if societies are making the wisest tradeoffs. The Times is embarking on this month's long project to explore the technology and where it's taking us, and to convene debate about how it can best help realize human potential."*

Privacy in Dispute? Convene a Debate? You're Kidding!

Only those in cryogenic freeze or in solitary confinement for the past couple of decades would not know that privacy is already dead, a quaint relic from a time long since past. In today's world, the price of participating in society is the sacrifice of privacy and self. It is not so much that technology is the culprit, it's that a networked world, whether through stories told around a campfire that are passed on in an oral tradition, or instantly via Facebook/Twitter, appears to be a necessary human craving. Wanting to belong to something or some group, to be able to identify with an ideology or fad is apparently irresistible.

What do you really have to trade with your fellow human beings other than your deepest secrets, knowledge and individuality?

Humans are merrily merging with machines or rather the software and interfaces that allow textual and vision immersion, and the light speed acquisition of knowledge that the networked world provides. The [Fourth Amendment](#) to the US Constitution be damned. Who needs it? The government or marketplace will always find a workaround to that relic of a bygone era.

All of this seems preordained by some Universal Machine God. We bow our heads whilst on the mobile device. The Internet/WWW is a sort of public confessional where there is no mediating priest to talk to God for you. It is straight talk with the Public God who dispenses likes or dislikes like the number of prayers a priest tells you to recite to regain a clean soul. And the Internet/WWW is a vengeful God with a long memory. Past sins from youth, or once though well hidden, find their way onto the network with punishment meted out by a hashtag with a name linked to it.

Sickness of the Future

The NYT Privacy Project, or even my musings here, are not necessary to understand future diseases at work right now in 2019.

For a better description of that we can turn to a short story written by Chinese Sci-Fi writer Chen Qiufan titled *"A **History of Future Illnesses**."* The story is located in the book *Broken Stars*, Contemporary Chinese Science Fiction in Translation (Ken Liu translator).

"Technology allows ritual to become an indivisible part of everyday life. Its implanted into you and becomes part of your genetic heritage to be passed on to your children and they children multiplying and mutating, more vigorous that its host. You cannot control the impulse to refresh the page. Information explosion brings anxiety but can fill your husk of a soul. Every fifteen seconds you move the mouse, open your social networking profile, browse the comments, retweet and reblog, close the page, and do it all over again fifteen seconds later. You can't stop.

You no longer talk to people in real life. Air has lost its role as the medium for transmitting voice. You sit in a ring, your eyes glued to the latest mobile device in your hand as though worshiping the talisman of some ancient god. Your thoughts now flow into virtual platforms at the tips of your fingers. You are auguring, laughing flustering joking. But reality around you is a silent desert.

You cannot free yourself from the control of artificial environments. Ritual is omnipresent. It is no longer restricted to sacrifice, sermon, mass, concert, or game performed on a central stage where the classical unities hold. Ritual itself is evolving, turning into distributed cloud computing, evenly spread out to every nook and cranny of your daily life. Sensors know everything and regulate the temperature, humidity, air currents and light around you; adjust your heart rate, hormonal balance, sexual arousal, mood. Artificial intelligence is a god: you think it is there for your welfare bringing you

*new opportunities, but you've
become the egg in the incubator,
the marionette attached to wires.
Every second of every minute of
every day, you are the sacrifice that
completes the unending grand
ritual. You are the ritual.*

*Radical thinkers obsess wove how to
withdraw from all this. The power
of ritual comes from repetition, not
its content. Day after day, the
repetition of poses and movements
gradually seeps into the depth of
consciousness like a hard drive's
read-write-head repeatedly tracing
the patterns of an idea, until the
idea becomes indistinguishable
from free will itself...Romantic love
is ritual's most loyal consumer
along with patriotism. The radicals
try to imitate the Luddites of old
[but]...the only thing that can be
done is nothing."*

War With North Korea: No Joke

The 20th Century Korean War from 1950-1953 pitting US-led United Nations coalition forces against the North Korean and Chinese militaries has been in pause mode for 64 years. The Korean Armistice was signed on July 27, 1953 by the United States, China and North Korea. It called for a cessation of hostilities until a lasting peace agreement between the warring parties could be negotiated and signed.

That, of course, has not happened due as much to North Korea's rationally maniacal behavior and ruthless treatment of its citizens, as to its role as a useful pawn of the Chinese and American governments. The Chinese feel compelled to let the incendiary North Korean government in Pyongyang irritate and provoke the United States and much of the world community, and the Americans don't mind having a large military presence to deter North Korea but also to keep an eye on China and the Southeast Asian region.

China has apparently reinforced its military forces on its border with North Korea.

Russia has a short land and maritime border with North Korea. In 2015 officials from the two countries signed an agreement to construct a road connection between the two neighbors during their "Year of Friendship." According to NK.News.org, North Korea and Russia envisioned "closer collaboration between the two states in political, economic and humanitarian spheres." As tensions ratchet up in the wake of North Korea's nuclear weapons and ballistic missile tests, Russia has apparently shored up its military forces near the bustling Russian port city of Vladivostok, home to Russia's Pacific Fleet and within range of North Korean missiles.

US-Led Coalition

These military moves by China and Russia make sense if war breaks out between a US-led coalition including South Korea, Japan, Canada, and Australia (for starters) and North Korean forces. The extra forces would likely be used to stanch the tide of North Koreans expected to stream out of North Korea. In the unfortunate circumstance that sees North Korea's first use of a nuclear weapon, a US retaliatory strike would ensure that the radiologically damaged would seek care in China and Russia, care that China and Russia can ill-afford to provide on a large scale.

During a protracted conventional conflict, it seems likely that enterprising organizations in China and Russia would attempt to funnel weapons and aid to the North Koreans to keep the US-led coalition occupied while they ponder their strategic and tactical options. With the US bogged down in Iraq, Syria and Afghanistan, there are many moves that the Chinese and Russians could make contrary to US interests.

The political and pundit classes in New York City and Washington, DC believe that the Trump Administration will just kick the Kim Jong-Un tin can down the road for another US president. The same elites told us all that Hillary Clinton would, with great certainty, win the 2016 presidential election. After 100 days of the Trump presidency, they still shake their heads in disbelief. Yet, they seemed to believe fully in President Trump's punitive April cruise missile strikes in Syria undertaken after a Bashar Al Assad use of a nerve agent on his own citizens.

But Trump's people say that the time for "strategic patience" with North Korea is over. Secretary of State Rex Tillerson, the Perry Como of the US State Department, declared as much during a recent visit to South Korea. Has America's new Ken and Barbie, Jared Kushner and Ivanka Trump, been advising President Trump on the matter?

As for China's influence, it has warned North Korea not to test Trump even as it recently resumed flights to North Korea from Beijing. Time will tell if China is serious in assisting the US or not.

Intellectuals?

Beyond the political and pundit classes who grace the world with their intellectual acumen are those across the spectrum who think that North Korea is the way it is because of the policies and practices of the US government. Those outlandish claims should not be seriously entertained. Kim Jong-Un can be seen in a video on YouTube smoking a cigarette and, at one point, sitting at a desk not far from an aircraft runway watching his air force and army in action. It looks a lot like a Monty Python skit until you realize that the North Koreans really believe they are a competent military power. And then there is the North Korean Army's recent live fire exercise. What kind of commanders and political leaders think that the compressed and massed alignment of artillery on a beach will deter US cruise missile strikes and other stand off weapons? The North Korean commanders are sentencing their troops to death using such arcane military practices. North Korean military doctrine is as obsolete as much of its weaponry is.

Still, war is horrible and North Korea would, initially, likely cause a lot of pain to the northern portions of Seoul, South Korea. US, South and North Korean civilian casualties would certainly follow. Pain reduction, not elimination, depends on the lethality of US preemptive missile, bomber and cyber-attacks designed to neutralize what the US-led coalition's intelligence believes to be the targets most important to hit first. Most likely, both North Korean nuclear weapons testing and medium-long range missile sites would be targeted, simultaneously with other North Korean conventional military assets.

Before such a conflict de-confliction lines with China and Russia would have to be opened.

The Fight

North Korea has to know that if it moves any weapons systems into the open, the heat or electronic emissions let off by those systems will be found and get them destroyed. US intelligence services have tried hard to anticipate how quickly the North Koreans can load and reload artillery and the extent of their ammunition supplies. Then there are the diesel submarines North Korea has in operation. US military antisubmarine warfare aircraft and detection is the best in the world and the Navy would be quick to begin the search for North Korean submarines. US attack class submarines would have to eliminate the DPRK's undersea threat very quickly, just as US air forces would be called upon to clear the airspace above North Korea as rapidly as possible. North Korean surface vessels would not do well against US anti-ship weaponry with its advanced guidance systems.

On the ground and from the sea, the situation is less clear. North Korea is vulnerable to amphibious landings on both its coastlines on the Yellow Sea and the Sea of Japan. The US Navy and Marine Corps would not attempt such landings until many days into a conflict though. North Korea is said to have sleeper cells in South Korea that would be activated to destroy key communications nodes and other critical infrastructure. North Korean Special Forces are said to be a dangerous threat as in any conflict they would be tasked with infiltrating South Korea to engage in sabotage.

It is not known how the North Korean civilian population would respond to an attack. The nation is home to 25 million people who have mostly known nothing but privation and austerity. Of course, that's the view from the outside. There are tantalizing hints that the civilians there might stay away from the fighting to a limited degree. Books smuggled out of North Korea like *The Accusation* give a hint of some of the thinking of the well-educated and economically better positioned denizens. But the US experience with insurgencies from Vietnam until the present have not been pleasant, successful affairs. At any rate, the "will" of the North Korean population would play a significant role in a protracted conflict.

Some argue that the US should learn from its 20th Century Korean War experience. But comparisons are invalid. The conflict took place as the US was drawing down from World War II and cold political winds were blowing. Since that time the North Koreans have spent a lot of time training to fight but have not been engaged in protracted conflicts for the last two decades as the US has been. There is no substitute for training but when military forces have experience in combat operations and maintain a training regime based on real-world fighting, there is going to be a mismatch at some point favoring the US.

Yet another consideration is the Joint Force capabilities of the North Korean military versus the US-coalition interoperability and joint force training. There is no evidence to suggest that North Korea has "networked" its fighting forces to wage war in the cross domains of sea, undersea, land, air, space and cyber. Nor has North Korea conducted extensive training exercises with partners or allies equivalent to Canada, Australia, Japan and South Korea.

No One Knows Plus that Unfinished Business Thing

A long term conflict in which the US-led coalition fails to bring North Korea to its knees would allow other nations to make risky moves. Would Russia invade Eastern Ukraine and move up to the Dnieper River? Would China move on Taiwan? Would Turkey move further into Syria? Would Iran move further into Syria and Iraq? Would Russia get more aggressive in Libya? Would Europe further splinter as some members of the European Union back the US while others do not (the UK would fight with the US)?

Would the American public support a longer term war effort?

Unfortunately, the US, North and South Korea issue is unfinished business. Not too many people on the planet want to see a video of the Kim Jong-Un of the future sitting at his portable desk smoking a cigarette while watching the North Korean "Death to America" ICBM successfully launched and carrying a nuke toward the United States.

If that ICBM made in through US missile defenses, the United States nuclear retaliatory response would turn North Korea into a radiological waste-land for decades. No one in the world wants to see that happen either.

The United States: A Nation on Suicide Watch

The Wars in Iraq and Afghanistan required major shifts in national resources from civilian to military purposes and contributed to the growth of the budget deficit and public debt. Through FY 2018, the direct costs of the wars will have totaled more than $1.9 trillion, according to US Government figures. Pollution is a serious issue. The United States (US) is a "large emitter of carbon dioxide from the burning of fossil fuels; deals with water pollution from runoff of pesticides and fertilizers; has limited natural freshwater resources in much of the western part of the country that require careful management. Deforestation; mining; desertification; species conservation; and invasive species (the Hawaiian Islands are particularly vulnerable) are widespread. Long-term problems for the US include stagnation of wages for lower-income families, inadequate investment in deteriorating infrastructure, rapidly rising medical and pension costs of an aging population, energy shortages, and sizable current account and budget deficits.

The onrush of technology has been a driving factor in the gradual development of a "two-tier" labor market in which those at the bottom lack the education and the professional/technical skills of those at the top and, more and more, fail to get comparable pay raises, health insurance coverage, and other benefits. But the globalization of trade, and especially the rise of low-wage producers such as China, has put additional downward pressure on wages and upward pressure on the return to capital. Since 1975, practically all the gains in household income have gone to the top 20% of households. Since 1996, dividends and capital gains have grown faster than wages or any other category of after-tax income... In December 2017, Congress passed and President Donald TRUMP signed the Tax Cuts and Jobs Act, which, among its various provisions, reduces the corporate tax rate from 35% to 21%; lowers the individual tax rate for those with the highest incomes from 39.6% to 37%, and by lesser percentages for those at lower income levels...The new taxes took effect on 1 January 2018; the tax cut for corporations are permanent, but those for individuals are scheduled to expire after 2025. The Joint Committee on Taxation (JCT) under the Congressional Budget Office estimates that the new law will reduce tax revenues and increase the federal deficit by about $1.45 trillion over the 2018-2027 period.

Are those the words of some left wing liberal publication or fake news from the mainstream media or conspiracy tinfoil hats? No, they are excerpts from the Central Intelligence Agency's (CIA) 2019 World Factbook, an unflinching look at all the planet's nations and their political systems, military expenditures, resources and internal and transnational troubles.

We're Number One! We're Number One!

Yes, indeed, the US has real problems, not imagined, as Republicans, Democrats and those with "Star Spangled Eyes" like to claim otherwise. "The US is the greatest country in history with the world's most powerful military. God Bless America!" they shout out or proclaim after every speech.

Perhaps at one point in history's past the nation had a shot to be the greatest of all time, at least in this solar system. Maybe that could have come after WWII, or the end of the Vietnam War, or even the largely successful Civil Rights movement. But now the country and its people are delusional in thinking that "everything's groovy".

What's to worry about? Gas prices are low, the National Football League season is underway and the Major League Baseball playoffs are just around the corner. What fun to watch these sporting events as military aircraft fly overhead and

20-something millionaires run around the baseball diamond or up and down the football field in stadiums, by the way, largely financed by the public. Who cares about lead infused water in Newark, New Jersey; Flint and Detroit, Michigan; and Pittsburgh, Pennsylvania?

And what can be said about the wars in Afghanistan, Iraq and Syria? Where's the victory to put in the US "Win" column? The American public has largely forgotten these tragic conflicts save those whose families have made a sacrifice. But sacrifice for what? Testing out new equipment, technology and war fighting doctrine? The War on Terror has siphoned off cash badly needed for US infrastructure repairs and has taken the lives of thousands of Americans.

Yes, it is correct that there has been no repeat of the 911 attacks, but the US is dealing with its own homegrown terrorist problem: active shooters. Is the US military going to start hunting them down here like they do Islamic State terrorists in the Middle East and Africa?

Hell on Earth

At any rate, the only maniacs who want US personnel to remain in Afghanistan, Iraq and Syria, three hell-holes created, in part, by the US, are zealous military leaders, defense contractors/suppliers, corrupt officials the US has propped up in the three countries, and black market operators eager to steal American weapons and sell them to the Taliban or groups like the Islamic State.

Oh, and let's not forget that Secretary of State Mike Pompeo (the Baron Harkonenn of the US government) and his boss President Donald Trump who are eager for war with Iran (which borders Iraq and Afghanistan, among other nations). That push has already started with the US exiting from the nuclear accord with Iran (Joint Comprehensive Plan of Action) in May 2018. The Trump administration has since unleashed punishing economic sanctions, and has adopted a blind-support policy for Israel and the bloodthirsty Saudis who would like nothing better than to have the US go to war with Iran. Yes, lets "do Iran" if not by direct military action then through subterfuge and dicey intelligence likely to be used to justify an ill-advised invasion.

The attack-Iran crowd has been singing the same old tune for at least 40 years now and it should have long ago been dust-binned. But here we are, again, moving toward the precipice of conflict.

According to the National Iranian American Council:

"The past 40 years in U.S.-Iran relations have been riddled with missed opportunities. While the Iranians and Clinton administration failed to initiate serious dialogue after Mohammad Khatami's election, the George W. Bush administration pocketed Tehran's assistance after the U.S. invasion of

Afghanistan, put the country in its "axis of evil," and ignored its offer for a grand bargain. Under the Trump administration, however, we are likely witnessing the greatest missed opportunity in four decades: a failure to capitalize on the Joint Comprehensive Plan of Action, aka the Iran nuclear deal."

War planners in the US have already sorted through all the airstrike contingencies and have plans, classified, of course, for air/missile strikes. But you need not wait for the day when the aircraft and missiles take to the skies over Iran and the talking heads from left, right and center media rant and rave about a brand new war, or retired generals show up to blather about this and that weapon system. Prepare yourself now. Be an educated armchair warrior by reviewing Anthony Cordesman's "Options in Dealing with Iran's Nuclear Program. It addresses the use of conventional and nuclear weapons by the US and Israel.

What's the Frequency, Kenneth?

It is commonplace for Americans to lionize US military leaders and look to them as calming voices, counterweights to warmongering government officials and their advisors. Ironic, isn't it? Can we look to our divine US military leaders to change the current thinking of the war hawks in the administration, congress and the think tanks that dot the Washington, DC Metro region?

Nope.

Consider this review by William Bacevich, a decorated combat veteran, of the newest US Central Command boss, Marine Corps General Kenneth McKenzie. McKenzie's area of responsibility (AOR) includes Iran.

General Kenneth McKenzie became the twenty-fourth commander of CENTCOM (more formally known as United States Central Command). On May 8, at an event sponsored by the Institute for the Perpetuation of War and the Promotion of Regime

Change, more formally known as the Foundation for the Defense of Democracies (FDD), he outlined his plans for building on the legacy of his 23 predecessors. None of those predecessors, it should be acknowledged, succeeded in accomplishing his assigned mission. Nor, I'm willing to bet, will he.

The essence of that mission, according to General McKenzie himself, is to promote stability. "A stable Middle East underpins a stable world," he announced, and "our steady commitment to our allies and partners provides a force for stability." As to how the region became unstable in the first place, he offers no opinion, leaving listeners with the impression that previous exertions by CENTCOM forces in invading, occupying, bombing, and otherwise spilling blood throughout his Area of Responsibility (AOR) had nothing to do with the absence of stability existing there today...This much seems clear: To listen to McKenzie, Iran is the ultimate source of all evil. To cite just one example, during Operation Iraqi Freedom, the general charges that "at least 600 US personnel deaths in Iraq were the result of Iran-backed militants." This was indeed nefarious, and one is hard-pressed to think of a comparable episode in recent military history, although US support for Saddam Hussein pursuant to his war of aggression against Iran might fill the bill."

Don't Bogart that Joint, My Friend

How are we faring in that other Long War, the War on Drugs?

The Office of National Drug Control and Policy (ONDCP) 2019 National Drug Control Strategy document describes the massive US local, state, and federal machinery set up to defeat drug trafficking organizations from getting their products to US streets and into the bodies of American citizens.

The High Intensity Drug Trafficking Areas (HIDTA) Program provides assistance to law enforcement agencies operating in areas determined to be critical drug-trafficking regions of the United States. HIDTAs provide an umbrella to coordinate Federal, state, local, and tribal drug law enforcement agencies' investigations, and act as neutral centers to manage, de-conflict, analyze, provide intelligence, and execute drug enforcement activities in their respective regions. With the recent inclusion of Alaska, the first new HIDTA in 17 years, the 29 regional HIDTAs now include designated areas in all 50 states, Puerto Rico, the US Virgin Islands, and the District of Columbia. The regional HIDTAs bring together more than 21,000 Federal, state, local, and tribal personnel from 500 agencies through 800 enforcement, intelligence, and training initiatives, all designed to disrupt illicit drug trafficking and dismantle criminal and drug trafficking organizations.

The US military, of course, plays a key role in the US War on Drugs, supporting HIDTA's among other activities. Take, for example, US

Southern Command's (SOUTHCOM) role in the Joint Interagency Task Force-South (JIATF-South). A 2005 briefing by former US Coast Rear Admiral Jeffrey Hathaway shows that no less than 14 agencies worked, and likely still do, chasing down illicit drugs in the SOUTHCOM AOR. These include the National Security Agency; the US Army, Air Force, Navy and Marines; the US Coast Guard, and the National Reconnaissance Office, among others. According to one of Hathaway's slides, every step involved in JIATF-South operations from interdiction to prosecution leads to intelligence. That is an interesting point. So 14 years later and all the intelligence collected has led to what, exactly?

Let's revisit the CIA's 2019 World Factbook for a read on how the War on Drugs effort is going. The US is the "world's largest consumer of cocaine (shipped from Colombia through Mexico and the Caribbean), Colombian heroin, and Mexican heroin and marijuana; a major consumer of ecstasy and Mexican methamphetamine; a minor consumer of high-quality Southeast Asian heroin; an illicit producer of cannabis, marijuana, depressants, stimulants, hallucinogens, and methamphetamine. It is also a money-laundering center."

Great!

This piece could go on and on citing data from a myriad of sources showing, among other things, the 500% growth rate of the US prison population, income inequality according to the Gini Coefficient which sees the US (41.5) right near Iran (40), or that one in six children in the US live in hunger. But, hey! The stock market is up, unemployment is down, and the dollar menu at McDonald's is fabulous.

The forever wars on Drugs and Terror, or the trumped up wars to come; income equality; homelessness; hunger, infrastructure collapse and the fracturing of US society into tribes is clearly a nationwide social,

political and cultural sickness:
perhaps mental illness. Even the
Internet/World Wide Web, once
viewed as a global unifying/
liberating force for change/good
has become what is termed the
Splinternet, reflecting large in-
group fanaticism, censorship and a
polarization of political beliefs. It is
now polluted with advertisements
just as radio and television are.

But there's still time left on the
clock to change the direction of the
country. Who or what will do that
and when it will happen I'm not
sure. But I take heart in Robert F.
Kennedy's insight below that there
are many who long to make "life
worthwhile" for everyone in
America, once again.

For Too much and too long, we
seem to have surrendered
community excellence and
community values in the mere
accumulation of material things.
Our gross national product...if we
should judge the United States of
America by that—counts air
pollution and cigarette advertising,

and ambulances to clear our highways of carnage. It counts special locks for our doors and the jails for those who break them. It counts the destruction of our redwoods and the loss of our natural wonder in chaotic sprawl. It counts napalm and the cost of a nuclear warhead, and armored cars for police who fight riots in our streets. It counts Whitman's rifle and Speck's knife, and the television programs which glorify violence in order to sell toys to our children.

Yet the gross national product does not allow for the health of our children, the quality of their education, or the joy of their play. It does not include the beauty of our poetry or the strength of our marriages; the intelligence of our public debate or the integrity of our public officials. It measures neither our wit nor our courage; neither our wisdom nor our learning; neither our compassion nor our devotion to our country; it measures everything, in short, except that which makes life worthwhile. And it tells us everything about America except why we are proud that we are Americans.

Trump and Supporters: Paranoiacs Following Lee Atwater's Racist Strategy

"He has been glorified as a hero and obeyed as a ruler, but fundamentally he is always the same. His most fantastic triumphs have taken place in our own time, among people who set great store by the idea of humanity. He is not yet extinct, nor will he ever be until we have the strength to see him clearly, whatever disguise he assumes and whatever his halo of glory. The survivor is mankind's worst evil, its curse and perhaps its doom. Is it possible to escape him, even now at this last moment?"
Elias Canetti, Crowds and Power

"[White] America's conscience is bankrupt. She lost all conscience a long time ago. Uncle Sam has no conscience. They don't know what morals are. They don't try and eliminate an evil because it's evil, or because it's illegal, or because it's immoral; they eliminate it only when it threatens their existence.

*So you're wasting your time
appealing to the moral conscience
of a bankrupt man like Uncle Sam.
If he had a conscience, he'd
straighten this thing out with no
more pressure being put upon him...
And in my opinion, the young
generation of whites, blacks,
browns, whatever else there is,
you're living at a time of
extremism, a time of revolution, a
time when there's got to be a
change. People in power have
misused it, and now there has to be
a change and a better world has to
be built, and the only way it's going
to be built—is with extreme
methods. And I, for one, will join in
with anyone—I don't care what
color you are—as long as you want
to change this miserable condition
that exists on this earth."* Malcolm
X, Oxford Union Debate, 1964

Canettii argues in his book that the
most dangerous individual holding
power is someone who views him/
herself as a Survivor, or someone
who can survive at the expense of
others. Canetti notes that the
Survivor, with access to nuclear

weapons, can obliterate a hefty chunk of mankind. The President of the United States, as Commander in Chief, has the option to use those weapons presumably only under the most dire of circumstances. President Donald Trump's proximity to the nuclear weapons trigger has been noted with trepidation by non-military observers from the beginning of his presidency and that matter is always lurking in the background, particularly as the US modernizes its Nuclear Triad. But the checks and balances in the use of the Nuclear Triad can't be discounted as it is likely that military commanders would refuse to carry out Trump's orders to use nukes even in spite of revised doctrine appearing to make it easier to do so.

The bigger problem, according to Canetti, is this: "Today, the survivor is himself afraid. He has always been afraid, but with his vast new potentialities his fear has grown too, until it is almost unendurable... The most unquestioned and therefore the most dangerous thing he does is to give commands."

Trump's world is a paranoid one. His apologists and supporters are loons. How else to describe those that refuse to condemn, even approve, racist presidential behavior. Trump and his disciples act as if they have survived some horrific mentally debilitating event; or indeed, expect one in the form of a color shift in America's complexion.

They fear the majority of the popular American electorate, they fear immigrants, they fear people of color, they fear LGBT's, they fear government funded social programs, they fear the questioning of their beliefs, and they fear non-Christians —and that's just for starters.

Didn't evolution weed these viruses out decades ago?

Trump and his disciples view themselves as a persecuted minority and that's dangerous because they really believe they are. The statistics, the demographics, show that Whites make up the largest chunk of the American population with Hispanics second at 18.3 percent and Blacks at 13.4 percent. Trump's people are horrified at the prospect that America will turn a light tinge of brown, which it inevitably will, by the 2050s and beyond.

Making Amends with Corporation and the Financial Sector

Trump is Canetti's Survivor, a hustler. He managed to gaming the legal and financial system to stay afloat, always getting rescued/supported by "his kind" for boneheaded business decisions and now for slashing US federal spending and regulations that protect the American public turning the US federal government into a bigger playground for corporations, businesses and interest groups (something corporations welcome with glee).

The Washington Post reported in 2016 that Trump declared Chapter 11 bankruptcy six times; four in the

1990s and two in the 2000s. In 2004, Trump's Hotel and Casinos Resorts was $1.8 billion in debt and couldn't meet its obligations.

So why do the corporate powerhouses of America stick with Trump even though he is a real estate swindler, racist and psychopath?

That's simple, he is repaying the corporate/financial world back for robbing them of billions of dollars years ago by giving them trillions now. He, and his Republican/ Democrat apologists in the US Congress, slashed corporate/ business tax rates, and they are now pillaging federal programs like the Supplemental Nutritional Assistance Program (SNAP) for budget cuts or elimination, ostensibly to save American taxpayers some money. Trump wants to drop 3.1 million people from SNAP.

It is the same story at the Environmental Protection Agency (EPA). According to the publication

Mother Jones, "On Wednesday [July 18], the United States Environmental Protection Agency doubled down on one of the most controversial environmental deregulation moves of the Trump presidency...the EPA reaffirmed its 2017 decision to reject a proposal from the agency's own scientists to ban an insecticide called chlorpyrifos that farmers use on a wide variety of crops, including corn, soybeans, fruit and nut trees, Brussels sprouts, cranberries, broccoli, and cauliflower."

And why would Trump be interested in chlorpyrifos that has been shown to be detrimental to children's brain development? "Dow AgroSciences' parent company, Dow Chemical, has also been buttering up Trump. The company contributed $1 million to the president's inaugural committee...the administration has approved the Dow-Dupont merger, and named several former Dow execs to high posts within the US Department of Agriculture," Mother Jones reported.

Just so.

Trump's Supporters: Theory of Evolution Apologizes Profusely

Trump lands uppercuts and left hooks to the American body politic and culture by ignorant Tweets that stoke racial tensions and non-partisanship.

Just how does a racist grifter, who tells four democratic congresswomen—Reps. Alexandria Ocasio-Cortez, D-NY, Ilhan Omar, D-MN, Ayanna Pressley, D-MA, and Rashida Tlaib, D-MI, to go back to their "totally broken and crime infested places from which they came" manage to win the support of millions of Americans and bump up Trump's poll numbers? Or why did 187 US House members vote not to condemn Trump's beliefs?

According to Pew Research, polling results for the 2016 election indicate that "Among the much larger group of white voters who had not completed college (44% of all voters), Trump won by more than two-to-one (64% to 28%)...Trump had an advantage among 50-to 64-year-old voters (51% to 45%) and those 65 and older (53% to 44%)."

And it is not just those who have not completed college or even attended college who are party of Trump's looney bin. Wealthy "smart" Republicans are part of the evolutionary mishap, as well. Republican CEO's side with Trump because he is helping them increase profit margins, shareholder dividends, and stock buybacks. What's all the fuss about a President of the United States who is both a racist and pro-business? It is, after all, just another write-off for the books.

According to a paper titled The Politics of CEO's, "We use Federal Election Commission (FEC) records to put together a comprehensive database of the political contributions made by over 3,500 individuals who served as CEOs of S&P 1500 companies during the period 2000-2017. We find that these political contributions display substantial partisan preferences in support of Republican candidates. To highlight the significance of CEO's partisan preferences for some corporate decisions, we show that public companies led by Republican CEOs tend to be less transparent to investors with respect to their political spending."

Senate and House Republicans, morally bankrupt to the core, are marching to the beat of a racist drummer.

Democrats: Remember Your Ugly History

The Democrats don't get a pass on racial issues. There's a lot for them to answer for as well.

Writing in The Hill, Burgess Owens notes that, "As a party with a history of pro-slavery, pro-secession, pro-segregation and pro-socialism, the Democratic Party has also been the party that has politically controlled urban black America for over 60 years.

Predominantly black communities in many cities today are mired in poverty, unemployment, illiteracy, crime and hopelessness. The Democratic Party has never apologized for its past, nor has it attempted to atone for its present failures.

Instead, it has skillfully used the art of bait-and-switch. Millions of Americans are convinced that somehow in the 1960s there was a wholesale transition of the Democratic Party's two-centuries-old hatred of black people to the policies of the anti-slavery, anti-secession, anti-segregation and pro-God Republican Party. Only in a vacuum void of common sense, critical-thinking skills and true American history could such logic survive."

Trump Channels Republican Lee Atwater

Former Republican National Committee Chairman Lee Atwater, known for his brutal, but successful, campaigning for Ronald Reagan and

George H.W. Bush, commented on flipping the Southern United States from racist Dixiecrats (Democrats) to, well, racist Republicans. Gone were the days of vulgar racist comments by Whites, and in came the days of using coded terms for racist policies.

In an interview with Atwater for a book on Southern party politics in 1981, while employed by the Reagan Administration, Atwater was asked this:

"But the fact is, isn't it, that Reagan does get to the [George] Wallace voter and to the racist side of the Wallace voter by doing away with legal services, by cutting down on food stamps?"

Atwater responded:

"Y'all don't quote me on this. You start out in 1954 by saying...By 1968 you can't say...that hurts you. Backfires. You say stuff like forced busing, states' rights and all that stuff. You're getting so abstract now [that] you're talking about cutting taxes, and all these things you're talking about are totally economic things and a byproduct of them is [that] blacks get hurt worse than whites. And subconsciously maybe that is part of it. I'm not saying that. But I'm saying that if it is getting that abstract, and that coded, that we are doing away with the racial problem one way or the other. You follow me—because obviously sitting around saying, "We want to cut this", is much more abstract than even the busing thing, and a hell of a lot more abstract than... So, any way you look at it, race is coming on the backbone."

And the beat goes on 38 years later.

Not All Whites

Many Whites have stood on the ramparts with people of color and other minorities to fight for equal rights and liberties. White judges and politicians have rendered decisions or passed legislation to turn the tide against racism in the USA. I'm not guilty of my Whiteness as I argued in

(Dissident Voice, 2015).

I know of no one, young or old, that likes to be pigeon-holed no matter their color, immigrant status, or their ethnic background. No one wins this type of blame game except the racists in Trump's camp who fan the flames of fear or those who mock the individuality of each human being.

So why are there racists out there in the open, in the White House, Congress, corporations and the voting public? What can be done about it?

I posed that question in 2015. I mean, should I attribute the sins of the world to Whiteness? Or should I conclude that the Species itself and the dominant economic and ruling methodology of Capitalism combine to make the "demon" that Ta-Nehisi Coates refers to and the "system" that Malcolm X wants us all to change: That American system, born largely of the British, Roman and Greek Systems, that relies on absurd contradictions and irony. A system that makes those from NWA and Straight Outta Compton, with all the female bashing lyrics, now part of the One Percent elite of corporate America; or the principals of the George W. Bush Administration clearly guilty of war crimes still cashing in on public office; or the poor and largely Black people that can't make $500 bail and waste away in jail; or the White miners in West Virginia killed because the mining company ignored safety rules and is found not guilty of negligence on a legal technicality; or the citizens of Detroit City denied, by a lone judge, the right to clean drinking water.

And what should I make of an American society that does not care about corporate surveillance (for profit) and government monitoring of all forms of communication (to maintain security and stability for the corporations to make profits)? Where were the White Rockers, Black Rappers, and Country Music stars when the wars in Iraq and Afghanistan raged on or the beach head for the corporate and government's invasion of privacy was the home?

They, all of them, were co-opted by a political, economic and cultural system we deny every day but in which we also live, procreate, operate and profit. With all of our complaints, we don't have a functional alternative to offer. The ballot-box provides no remedy. Presidential and Congressional elections are polluted by money and interests, foreign and domestic, over which voters have no control. Politicians are bought and sold like horses prior to a race.

I don't think I'm White. I think I am a human being. I don't know what it is like to be rich and in the top 20 percent of money makers in the USA. I know that I'm color-labeled as White and class-labeled as Middle by the identity and false consciousness hunters that roam the American landscape.

I know I agree with Dave Chappelle, famed comedian with $10 million in the bank, who is labeled as Black and Wealthy. But I'm not a smart guy and I think that he is a human being and a really funny guy with great observations of the human condition. I think that way of George Carlin, Chris Rock and the late Robin Williams. According to Chappelle "I support anyone's right to be who they want to be. My question is: To what extent do I have to participate in your self-image?"

I don't want to participate in the self-image, the evolutionary mishap, that is President Donald Trump, his apologists and his supporters. I also don't want to deal with duplicitous Democrats who always seem ready to enable Trump's foolishness.

It seems to me there is no vocal, turbulent opposition to the madness that permeates the United States of America these days. Who inspires any longer? Who can compromise?

Who will fight?

America's Education System: Teaching the Price of Everything and the Value of Nothing

"Ask students to read for more than a couple of sentences and many will protest that they can't do it. The most frequent complaint that teachers hear is that it's boring. It is not so much the content of the written material that is at issues here; it is the act of reading itself that is deemed to be boring. What we are facing here is not just time-honored teenage torpor, but the mismatch between a post-literate New Flesh that is too wired to concentrate and the confining concentrational logics of decaying disciplinary systems. To be bored means simply to be removed from the communicative sensation-stimulus matrix of texting, YouTube and fast food; to be denied, for a moment, the constant flow of sugary gratification on demand. Some students want Nietzsche in the same way they want a hamburger; the fail to grasp—and the logic of the consumer system

encourages this misapprehension— the indigestibility, the difficult is Nietzsche." Mark Fisher, Capitalist Realism: Is There No Alternative?

I am a substitute teacher (grades K-12) in a public school system located in Virginia, a state on the eastern seaboard of the United States. For many years prior to becoming a substitute teacher, I also taught at a private school in Virginia. Tuition and fees at the private school are approximately $42,000 (USD), the public schools are, of course, tuition free.

To be sure, there are highly motivated students in both educational settings that call into question Mark Fisher's observation above. But in the main, both organization's struggle with figuring out if they are working with their subjects as students or as consumers of services provided by teachers and administrators.

From what I have observed in the tiny microcosm in which I've worked, adults have not figured out how to teach Generation Z. It is as if K-12 students are; well, lab rats, in a messy experiment that reflects adult confusion about how to facilitate learning in an era when all the "book learning" education seeks to impart is largely available on the World Wide Web (WWW). Reality hits video screens before adults can interpret it for their children; that is, assuming the adults are up to the task. Twitter, a modern day ticker-tape, dumbs down the American populace. Attention spans for students and adults are measured in 10 minute increments, if that.

Teachers are little more than circuits in America's educational network and, as such, transmit surface information to the students and little more. The kids know a lot, for sure, but they, like the adults that school them and lead them, have no intellectual depth, something required for critical thinking. It is fitting, I suppose, that in these times when the United States is a polarized nation of cynics who believe in nothing, it's not surprising that its educators teach the young to be cynics. But as Oscar Wilde noted through one of his characters, a cynic is "one who knows the price of everything but the value of nothing."

And yet the very adults (academics, corporate leaders, politicians) that created this cynical, digitized short attention span world whine about students not being able to read and write, think critically or master math. There is a reason for that: They are not being taught effectively to do those things. All of which reaffirms something I wrote in 2013: The American Education System is creating Ignorant Adults.

The leaders of Boeing and Lockheed Martin worry out loud about the absence of US school aged students who can excel at science, technology, engineering and math disciplines (STEM). But they have no problem funding initiatives for Chinese students and aviation professionals in China.

Hocus Pocus

Back in the USA, school classrooms are a mishmash of technology, new wave/repackaged learning techniques and revisionist history. Apple I-Pads and Smart Boards are located in each classroom for student/teacher use. They are all connected to software that provides music, cartoons and learning platforms like Canvas for most grade levels. The latest teaching fads like Maker Learning with its "Digital Promise" backed by Google and Pixar, among others, competes with concepts like the Flipped Classroom, Blended Learning and other pedagogies that come in and out of vogue. And yet, alongside all the technology are crayons, magic markers, pencils, paper and cardboard for writing and drawing.

It's no stretch to say that I-Phones, Android and other handheld devices may cause epigenetic changes. Students, teachers/coaches and administrators are constantly staring head down at their computing-communications devices. It is tough to get a face-to-face conversation going with most anyone in these groups as their eyes and heads are in the down position while sitting, walking or standing. Even if you are having a meatspace meeting, participants will incessantly dart their eyes to the handheld safely nearby the hand, in the hand, or on the lap (looking down again).

America's past, woeful in many respects, is being revised again by adults to suit the agenda of those who seek to promote a narrative that seeks to change the political/cultural narrative of US society and its history, and it is aimed at young students in particular. The New York Times (NYT) 1619 Project is an example of this. According to the World Socialist Website, "The 1619 Project, launched by the Times in August, presents American history in a purely racial lens and blames all white people for the enslavement of 4 million black people as chattel property. "

The NYT has provided teaching materials that are being used by colleges, universities and high schools across the United States. Who is willing or capable of debating the claims of the New York Times; or should we say, who is willing to be labeled a racist for disagreeing with The revisionist authors of the 1619 Project? At the collegiate level, at least, there may be debate on the matter but at the high school level, what teacher is going to argue against using 1619 teaching materials. After all it *is* the New York Times.

What is very troubling about the NYT revisionism is that it makes the preposterous claim that racism is part of the DNA of all white people. The World Socialist Website claims that: "This is dangerous politics, and very bad history...[it] mixes anti-historical metaphors pertaining to biological determinism (that racism is printed in a "national DNA") and to religious obscurantism (that slavery is the uniquely American "original sin"). But whether ordained by God or genetic code, racism by whites against blacks serves, for the 1619 Project, as history's deus ex machina. There is no need to consider questions long placed at the center of historical inquiry: cause and effect, contingency and conflict, human agency and change over time. History is simply a morality tale written backwards from 2019."

Sharpen My Pencils, Fool!

I have often winced at some of the practices I observed in classrooms. On a typical day as a substitute, I arrive at a school, pick up instructions left by the teacher who is absent (or has a meeting), and head to the classroom. Substitute teachers, or Subs, are a lower class of species, members of the gig economy, and treated as such by the "real" teachers and students. I remember one teacher I subbed for was headed off to a meeting and as she left said, "Sharpen my pencils for me." I dutifully did. A majority of the teachers and administrators don't ask for your name, you're just known as "The Sub."

Once students complete their work (if they even choose to do it), which for most does not take much class time, they are free to play video games, stick earbuds in and listen to music or hang out with friends via the handheld device. One of the popular video games with male 6th to 12th graders is Krunker, a first person shooter game. Is US society really that concerned about active shooters in schools?

The State and corporations can be found in some form in the public school system. One elementary school has Lockheed Martin as a sponsor of a science program. In another elementary school, a class is learning about Virginia's geography: The students print and video work product will ultimately be used by a tourism association in the State.

In both institutions learning is calibrated to the SAT, ACT and various Advanced Placement tests. Student test scores serve as one metric for teacher performance reviews along with standards set by school boards, the State, or independent audits in the private school case.

Students are not required to stand or even pay attention to the United States Pledge of Allegiance that is carried via intercom into the classrooms each morning. Some schools don't even bother with it. Yet, during sporting events like American contact football, students/athletes and fans are required, or let's say by the pressure of custom are compelled, to stand for the playing of the United States' National Anthem. American flags are stitched into football jerseys and prior to games one football player is selected to run the American flag onto the field amidst the adrenaline fueled shouts and growls of fellow teammates following close behind. A color guard from a high school's junior reserve officer training corps (JROTC) sometimes is present. They present in strict marching formation the American flag along with the flags of the US Navy, Marine Corps and Air Force.

To stand and recite the Pledge of Allegiance in a classroom takes one minute. To be upright for the National Anthem takes, perhaps, five minutes. The school band normally plays the latter and on occasion high school Madrigals will sing the National Anthem.

Yes, the militarization of US society and the deification of military personnel, even if they are accountants in uniform working at the Pentagon, is something to be concerned about. But saying the Pledge, and standing for the National Anthem, should be a requirement for students. There has to be some measure or display of loyalty to one's country and the young must learn that. Still many want to wipe away any sense of citizenship, patriotism. Well, they are doing a fine job of that.

Mind the Inmates!

Students at both institutions are the beneficiaries of some serious force protection measures normally associated with protecting military personnel stationed at installations around the globe. The public schools in which I worked have armed police officers on site with a phalanx of civilian security/disciplinarians roaming the halls. Security cameras are everywhere indoors (hallways) and outside (entry and exit) recording movements. Public school buses are also outfitted with cameras and tracking systems.

The private school where I was once employed uses a less blunt force approach opting for a more subtle presence: security personnel are a bit less obvious and do not carry firearms. The school does employ a corporate style full-time director of security and safety with some serious emergency management credentials.

It is the same security scene at public and private schools across the United States which raises an interesting question: Are students really captive minds in minimum security enclosures subjected daily to social, emotional learning techniques or socialization/habilitation for entry into society? Or are they "free" learners allowed to be creative and explore beyond the confines of the pedagogy that seeks to "standardize" them.

No Student Untracked

There is a functioning big data brother at work tracking students as they make their way through K-12 known as the Common Core of Data (CCD). CCD is described by Marc Gardner in a presentation for the US National Center for Education Statistics (NCES)as "the annual collection of the universe of United States public elementary, secondary education agencies and schools. Data include enrollment by grade, race/ethnicity and sex, special education, english learners, school lunch programs, teachers, dropouts and completers." The CCD also gathers information from state justice, health and labor departments. The NCES also collects data from private schools.

It doesn't end there. Colleges and universities are tracking high school seniors as they begin their searches for schools they'd like to attend. The Washington Post recently reported that many colleges and universities have hired data capture firms to track prospective students as they explore websites. "Records and interviews show that colleges are building vast repositories of data on prospective students — scanning test scores, zip codes, high school transcripts, academic interests, web browsing histories, ethnic backgrounds and household incomes..."

The owner of Canvas, referenced above, is Instructure. Their mission, according to their investor website is to "grow [the young] from the first day of school to the last day of work [retirement]." One of the capabilities that Instructure provides its clients is Canvas Folio Management. According to the investor webpage, it "delivers an institutional homepage and deep, real-time analytics on student engagement, skills and competencies, network connections, and interactions across various cohorts. Allows institutions to generate custom reports tied directly to student success initiatives and export accreditation-ready reports on learning outcomes at the student, cohort, course, program, or institutional level."

Ah, yes, the thrill of being hunted for a lifetime by big data brother. Anyway, there is no escape.

Don't try this in a Classroom

"Learning is an active process, not simply a matter of banking information in a recipient's passive mind. Teaching therefore has to be a transactional process rather than just the transmission of information. The transactional aspect is essential to enabling students to challenge their situations in life, which they must learn to do if they are to play their parts as active citizens of a better world...teaching must be approached as an intellectually disruptive and subversive activity if it is to instill inquiry skills in learners and encourage them to think for themselves rather than mindlessly accept received ideas. We believe it is more important in the digital age than ever before." (Ingenious: The Unintended Consequences of Human Innovation by Peter Gluckman and Mark Hanson, Harvard Press)